MW01515945

Dearest Laurie, *January 2021*

WHERE ARE YOU FROM, ORIGINALLY?

My sweet soul sister, I hope you enjoy these!

☆
☆ ☆
☆ ☆
☆ ☆

With love,

poems by

Joy Arbor

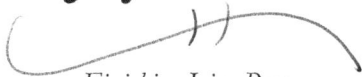

Finishing Line Press
Georgetown, Kentucky

WHERE ARE YOU FROM, ORIGINALLY?

ACKNOWLEDGMENTS

Grateful acknowledgment is made to the following publications in which these
poems first appeared:

Crab Orchard Review: "Berlin Snapshots" and "Where Are You From,
Originally?"
Hayden's Ferry Review: "Trying to See the Diner"
24 Pearl: The Magazine: "Napping in Jerusalem"
Dunes Review: "Instead of Buying Another Fifth"
Natural Bridge: "Sacramento Delta"

Editor: Christen Kincaid

Cover Art: Unknown, Augsburger Wunderzeichenbuch, Folio 65 (Comet mit
einem grosen Schwantz, 1401)

Author Photo: Robert O'Brien

Cover Design: Elizabeth Maines

Printed in the USA on acid-free paper.
Order online: www.finishinglinepress.com
           also available on amazon.com

Author inquiries and mail orders:
Finishing Line Press
P. O. Box 1626
Georgetown, Kentucky 40324
U. S. A.

Table of Contents

For my grandparents,
Harry and Zipora Levin,
Bonnie Ross and Ben Ard,
of blessed memory

And for Robert and Sean

Storyteller Hyakutake

watching you travel the northern sky in March, 1996

You must tell our story.
That once we stopped
long enough to see you,
a remnant of creation, hurling
through darkness with the headlights
of countless suns in your eyes.
We saw, we were there, we existed.
We fasten this to you, Hyakutake,
a barrette for your hair, a souvenir
of us and this Earth.

And in 10,000 years, which of Earth's eyes
will be blooming and happen to see
you, Hyakutake, and your hair
burning with the stories of the universe?

Where Are You From, Originally?

A game about belonging.
Who you are in the names of countries.
First, an American game—whoever

stepped off the Mayflower
won. Later, proud to call ourselves Indian,
that something in us did not steal

this land but grew from it
native as the plains.

Some stories were too complicated. Berlin
seemed easy, but Germany was a late invention,
and as Jews we were always from somewhere else—

an ancestor expelled from Spain. Shifting borders,
shifting names Czechoslovakia, then emigrated
to Palestine, the War for Independence—Israel. Oh why

emigrate then, after that language
of conquerors was thrown off and demand your children
swim against sharks? In the US, that my father couldn't

be President and had hair that no ski-cap could tame
couldn't be mitigated by the blondest shiksa,
her Heinz 57 of Quakers and Cherokee princess claims.

I cannot name myself
through nations—my family not blood American,
to be Israeli is to be from somewhere else in a language

I don't know, to be a Jew is to be everywhere
shuttled across borders, to meet at the borders
with the family from the other side, to escape

across borders—Czech, Poland, Germany, Spain.
To be half-Jewish from the wrong parent?
Hitler would round me up. Israel wouldn't bury me.

Hebrew

I'm a little girl trying to still my flapping
arms. Grandma speaks to her friends
and points. They nod, ken, ken. I nod
but don't understand. At the dinner table
Grandma lapses. Grandpa bellows: *speak
English, woman. This is America!*
                              Years later,
we're shopping. She overhears
what? a whisper? an accent?
whole words like dates in her mouth,
the language her parents spoke to her last.
She interrupts the stranger, instant friends.
They'll get together for tea and chat
about Tel Aviv. I pretend to be fascinated
by pet store chameleons.
                    For centuries, women were
taught only enough to manage the twice-daily
prayers. The rabbis spoke Hebrew when they
didn't want women or those-like-women
to hear. My family speaks Hebrew when
they don't want the kids to understand.
Only Grandma can write.
                    My father says
he sometimes thinks in his first language. A linguist
in a supermarket checkout line catches
traces of accent.
                    When Grandpa was sixteen, lucky
orphan refugee on a bug-infested kibbutz in Haifa,
he didn't know Hebrew. English was the language
of the colonizer; German soon the enemy's
language.

Eliezer Ben-Yehuda insisted his wife
speak only Hebrew to their son. When
at four, the boy still hadn't spoken, she sang
in Russian. Eliezer roared and the first word
screeched out of the first Hebrew child:
Abba.
    Zionist linguists hammered away
forging the language of Torah and the Song of Songs
on the anvil of the modern
world, on tractors and iceboxes.
Only women could resuscitate it, their breath
bursting the desert husk into blossom.
Women speaking Hebrew heralded
the revolution.
        In my father's headlong rush
to stop being the smelly Jew, he didn't teach me,
but years later, he and his cousins yammer away
beseder, beseder in their big houses
in the Valley.
        My grandmother's mind shorting out,
she shouts to me
    ani ohevet otach ani ohevet otach ani ohevet otach.

Berlin Snapshots
for my grandfather

When he returned, a war-aged twenty-four,
to the streets he'd last seen at sixteen, his home
had become a gas station, his parents—
twin map locations. Now, a half-century
later, nothing wears a number 71 on this street,
nor is there an empty space between fences.

Still standing is the brownstone he left
as a boy, its face lined with scaffolding.
We feel our way up dim winding floors.
Two flights up, I blink into the light
of the planning office; he thinks
he's found the flat where he was born.

He points to a wide pane—here,
in his day, a terrarium had housed red geraniums
(though he can't recall the English word,
describing its dimensions of glass walls
with an engineer's precision).

I pose on the step by the too-bright windows.
He stands back far enough
to catch in the frame the empty
floor where in his memory he carries
a knife and is forever falling.

He says he still has the scar.
The flash doesn't go off. But by his parents'
dull black headstones, stiff and straightbacked as he
against Weissensee's underbrush—*smile now, smile*—
the flash singes.

Grandpa's Visit with Eva, Munich, 1997

Her stories wind themselves
around her legs, weigh down her shopping net.

He's trekked a half century to collect them—
which neighbors shrank away to work camps

the date she was released from Theresienstadt,
that his aunt didn't die from disease

but conviction and a cure only a daughter
could administer. She scraped along sewers

and tombs in Germany the rest of the war.
She'd rather her kaffee und kuchen

were praised, antiques appreciated. He escaped
to the Promised Land. Alone,

with no pictures or letters. She says
Nazis murdered his parents—when the orders

came, they gassed themselves in their home.
She stammers and stutters. She'd rather forget

holding her breath behind false walls.
His eyes are famished, his need

raw. He's forgotten there's a future
to save for, pen poised above the page.

Rising from the Bed

I walk the old house
sometimes shuffling
down the stairs so fast I forget

I haven't lived
here in years.
The sleeping family

twitches and starts.
All their changes fade; the original house
bleeds through.

Perhaps their ghosts prowl
former homes, the present cracking open
to fix what they remember.

The cords that join every day to dream
twist and tangle.
Some memories jump from line to line.

Searching for Uncle Dicker, Savignyplatz, Berlin
Siegfried Buchold (1863-1932)

Three mornings, a traveler's small eternity,
I've tried to see Grandpa's Great-Uncle Dicker

With his dachshunds and newspaper, his tired hat,
Bickering with other pensioners as Grandpa said he'd be

Here at Savignyplatz, an eden bisected by traffic, while morning
Glories blaze, the now-chic neighborhood held back and beeping.

But so early in the morning only bums doze
Through the chill and the U-Bahn's rumbling.

A woman stares straight out as if something
Were calling for her from her own foggy breath.

I can see Dicker, Fatso, only as Grandpa
Did, waving and bicycling past

To something else—a desert adventure,
A promise of pastry or pocket money.

No wonder Grandpa can't tell me what made Dicker
Thought was worth arguing about. Isn't aging

Entering the same room from a different door?
Now Grandpa is the man near the end of his life

Struggling to remember what old age looks like from the beginning.
Now I am the one who. . .
                             steamy coffee, stiff wool, I trudge

Across cobblestone, phantom dogs nipping
Bony ankles, an illusion so real I almost

Fall. The morning glories have died
Back. I inch my way

Down to the bench, distrusting my bones to impact.
There'll be a bruise there tomorrow. It's winter.

I spread my *Berliner Zeitung*
Over my legs, open myself to the sad news

Of a world already given over to uniforms again.
Nothing left to do but to shake my head.

I could get used to this—dress in the cold dark
The walls full of snores from countless other rooms,

Emerge as gray loses its grip on the sky,
Rage with other survivors of war and time,

Die long before crashed glass, upturned homes,
Broken stores, neighbors disappearing

Into night, narrow bed barracks, marches,
Millions set aflame, before ash becomes our air

Before children shrug at history's gruesome tales

With the Big Bad Wolf and the Boy Who Cried,
Plodding under this legacy of drenched wool.

Yes, to be erased before these benches
Are painted in careful green script

Nicht für Juden.

You're going along fine

and then your past places its
claws on your shoulder, canines
slipping into your neck as if sinew
and bone are butter—before you can stop it, before you can
defend yourself with distraction, its poison
spreads like an anesthetic,
like water overwhelming a riverbed, like your sleep's
dead weight propelling you down
through the sheets and mattresses
and wood floor, pressing deep into loamy
earth, the twining of dreams
for a blanket. You try to
lift yourself out, like trying to jump lying down, like
running through mud, and only
little by little the roots and vines
loosen and pull and untangle and you
swim yourself up out of it,
snapped ends of memories
sticking to you with sap.

After

Daily, we blink our eyes open into harsh morning.
How is it that we don't squeeze them shut again,
rush back into the blissdrug of sleep?
The Holocaust scorches everything
blisters every deed.
Why live if we cannot learn?
Bosnia, Rwanda, Afghanistan, Darfur.
Some days—memory bores into my skull.
Others—having passed through a breezeway
of forgetting, I am washing piled dishes,
shoving clothes into drawers, and the Shoah
taps its cane
above my right eye.
Is it any wonder I want to rejoin the here and now
drink and get high and have sex?
What can I ever do to repay
the debt of surviving,
offset your dying—
live more, be more worthy?
Tell me what you'd do—
smell lilacs all day long,
savor brisket and prime rib,
wander in the open air, marveling
at a sky not hemmed in by bars?
How do I make good
so it can't happen, or doesn't, or happens
less often—a thousand deaths a day for one hundred days?
Tell me how to live without being charred.

Trying to See the Diner

Sometimes, when I think of the news—
an old man stabbed in his home, children
                    whose chests
are pummeled with hunger or work,
                    fathers dipping
into their daughters, mothers past boiling point—

I try to think of sitting at a diner
the order of the flatware—fork,
                    knife, spoon—
how everyone knows that especially
the spoons will bend far back, since they can,
                    before breaking.
But many people refrain. And I think of
the simple exchange: I give you a
                    dollar
and you lay down
a cup of coffee, all the cream I need.
I ask for toast
and unlike peace or luck or safety, you
can bring it, you can
put it in front of me
because I want it and I can
push it away when
                    I don't.

But even here, beside me,
just outside the glass—small hands, screaming.
A young girl shaking a torrent of hair,
low rumbling through the floor.
                    Behind her,
a mother. The girl is
                    yanked away.

I wonder if she will ever
                    let her mother have
her arm, let her rip it
                    right off
and get away.

Napping in Jerusalem

Voices cross
    the threshold of your sleep.

Not your father's reluctant Shabbat prayers
    before blaring "let's eat,"

not your mother's murmurs
    echoing deep in the canals of memory.

Not song rising from the *wadi*
    women hanging their washing,
    lines criss-crossing yards
    below your high window.

The adhan calls Al-Qud to its knees.

The Old City a breeze
    sneaking in your Mount Scopus room.

Above your narrow bed,
    with honks and pop music,
    not Shema Yisrael,
    but Asr Salah
    steals into your dreams.

Instead of Buying Another Fifth
for your birthday

come to the bookshop—the sky's shaking
out sheets of rain onto the cars, your car,
you, as you cross and dodge the lot

of smeared streetlights and carlights and cars, trapped
inside yourself and your sweaters and thoughts.
Be glad you made it, made it through

though your marriage is creaking
to a close, your father is coughing up blood,
a man has died you thought you knew.

Open the door. Store-heat heaves
itself over you. You can have all

of this. What answer hasn't come here
to be stored? Surely one of these dead voices can
crowd out your own for a while,

until you stop, look up, turn the
page, reminded things will never be
the same by something suddenly

appearing or gone. You could go on
for months like this, buying stacks and stacks
memorizing the cashiers by name

and shift, storing up enough words so
when split open and forced to speak,
none are yours.

This is commerce—
in this same-price-for-all
democracy as long as you can pay, you pay

the current exchange rate for your time,
and time, all you have and can barter,
all you're looking to pass anyway.

What It Means to Survive

Another deer beside the road, head
severed neatly from its body.
A squirrel is split, skin

peeled, a full-body
autograph. The deer is left to dry
out—the regress of skin to bone

on the shoulder of the highway.
There, at the side of the road, we watch
ourselves drive by.

It's me who's been caved in
and a white-tailed doe is behind the wheel
hoof to the gas, speeding

off, saying a little prayer
for the return of my body to the earth.
The heap of me smirks;

she knew it would be that easy, snaps
her broken neck in place, straps
a hubcap to her shattered knee and

moves on,
slowly, into the woods
favoring one leg.

Sacramento Delta

In places where rivers meet, people stall
waterlogged, the air sticky with dreams.

In patches of sun, we hang ourselves
out to dry, to remember
simple things: clothes, food, TV.

Within boundaries, we can do dishes,
type memos, avoid sleep,
while longing peels paint from the walls.

Even gulls fly slowly
working the sky like honey.

Morning Commute on Route 23

Breath clings
to the trees, a sea
suspended,

the oakleaf of soaring geese
barely visible above.
The farthest blue

distances of sky,
once so open,
have lowered on us,

a cocoon of mist
keeping us to ourselves,
what's within, invisible.

We speed through it,
my son and I, to another day of doing,
machine-like, impervious.

Through car windows our glimpse
of the wild, holy world as it is,
as we are,

a voice everchanging,
summer's screech sighing
into November's hush.

Additional Acknowledgments

With tremendous appreciation to Christine Stewart-Nuñez, who gave me the great gift of her considerable help and support in putting this chapbook together. Without Christine, this chapbook would not exist.

With appreciation also to the many people who gave supportive and constructive feedback on these poems (and my apologies to those I've forgotten): Chana Bloch, Elmaz Abinader, Yiskah Rosenfeld, Frances Sackett, Eileen Ferrari, Hilda Raz, Amber Harris Leichner, Tim Lepczyk, Drucilla Wall, Dean Young, and Cyrus Cassells.

With thanks also to Carolyn Forché, whose workshop exercise gave me "Morning Commute on Route 23."

With thanks to Elizabeth Maines for designing such a beautiful cover.

With my deepest thanks to my wonderful bashert, Robert, and our beautiful son, Sean, for their love and support.

Joy Arbor was born and raised in Los Angeles, California and got her BA at California State University, Northridge. Then she moved, getting an MFA in Creative Writing from Mills College in Oakland, California, and moved several more times before earning her PhD at University of Nebraska-Lincoln. After a semester at the American University in Cairo (Egypt) and a year in her native Los Angeles, where her son was born, she and her family moved to Michigan, where they are now happily rooted in Columbiaville.

Her poems have been published or are forthcoming in *Natural Bridge*, *Crab Orchard Review*, *Hayden's Ferry Review*, and *Jewish Currents* among others. Her poems have been awarded the Gaffney/Academy of American Poet's Prize, the Mary Merritt Henry Prize, and the Phenomena of Place Poetry Prize as well as a Writer's Grant from the Vermont Studio Center. She is an associate professor of communication at Kettering University in Flint, Michigan where she teaches communication and ethics. In her free time, she gardens and gazes at the muskrats collecting cattails in the pond.

CPSIA information can be obtained at www.ICGtesting.com
Printed in the USA
BVOW08s2248210316

441240BV00001B/2/P